Decorating with Seashells

Decorating with Seashells

Anita Louise Crane

Sterling Publishing Co., Inc. New York
A Sterling/Chapelle Book

Chapelle Limited

Owner: Jo Packham

Design Director: Linda Curtis

Staff: Areta Bingham, Kass Burchett, Marilyn Goff, Holly Hollingsworth, Susan Jorgensen, Kimberly Maw, Barbara Milburn, Linda Orton, Karmen Quinney, Leslie Ridenour, Cindy Stoeckl, Gina Swapp, Sara Toliver

Photography: Kevin Dilley for Hazen Imaging, Inc.
        Scott Zimmerman for Scott Zimmerman Photography
Photo styling: Anita Louise Crane
Copy written by: Jo Packham

Library of Congress Cataloging-in-Publication Data Available

10   9   8   7   6   5   4   3   2   1

Published by Sterling Publishing Company, Inc.
387 Park Avenue South, New York, N.Y. 10016
© 2001 by Anita Louise Crane
Distributed in Canada by Sterling Publishing
c/o Canadian Manda Group, One Atlantic Avenue, Suite 105
Toronto, Ontario, Canada M6K 3E7
Distributed in Great Britain and Europe by Cassell PLC
Wellington House, 125 Strand, London WC2R 0BB, England
Distributed in Australia by Capricorn Link (Australia) Pty Ltd.
P.O. Box 6651, Baulkham Hills, Business Centre, NSW 2153, Australia
Printed in China
All rights reserved

Sterling ISBN 0-8069-3639-8

If you have any questions or comments, please contact:
Chapelle Ltd.
P.O. Box 9252
Ogden, UT 84409

(801) 621-2777
Fax (801) 621-2788
chapelle@chapelleltd.com
www.chapelleltd.com

For Ellen.
i love you mom.

I would like to thank my editor for her dedication and creative talent in producing this lovely book. I would also like to thank all the staff at Chapelle for their help and support, especially Jo Packham for giving me this opportunity to express my artistic abilities in every project, photograph, and illustration. A special thank you to my husband Bruce for living with a house full of seashells on every conceivable surface in our home during the creative process.

I would also like to thank Tricia Dalglish for the beautiful shell lights on pages 56–57 and 134; Kathy Pace for the creative vest adorned with carved shell buttons on page 40, shell pincushion on page 12, and the little castle surrounded with tiny seashells on page 64; and Kim Streit for the shell-filled vases on pages 34 and 117, the shell trees on page 55, the shell centerpiece on page 130, and gift bags on page 136.

I would like to offer my sincere appreciation of the valuable support given in this ever-changing industry of new ideas, concepts, designs, and products. Several projects shown in this publication were created with the outstanding and innovative products developed by:

Other books by Anita L. Crane:

Teddy Bear Magic

Two-Hour Teddy Bears

Two-Hour Dolls' Clothes

Making Adorable Teddy Bears

Adorable Furniture for Dolls and Teddy Bears

Two-Hour Scrap Crafts

Dubin Ceramics
Lygia Dubin
2955 Laguna Canyon Rd. #8
Laguna Beach, CA 92651
(949) 497-5682

Ercole, Inc. Showroom
116 Franklin St.
New York, NY 10013
(212) 941-6098

Gooseberry Hill Notions
1-800-698-6576

Pfaff American Sales Corp.
P.O. Box 566
Paramus, NJ 07653-0566
(201) 262-7211

Phoebe Lantini Design
586 Utah St.
San Francisco, CA 94110
(415) 863-8056

Plaid Enterprises, Inc.
P.O. Box 117600
Norcross, GA 30091-7600
(770) 923-8200

Ginger Sizemore
enchantedfantasies.com/treasure.html
e-mail: ginger@aloha.net

Walnut Hollow
1409 State Road 23
Dodgeville, WI 53533
(800) 950-5101

A special thank you to Joanie Howell, Park City, UT; Kathy Pace, Coalville, UT; Dixie Barber, Park City, UT; Jo Packham, Ogden, UT; and Susan Ure, Salt Lake City, UT, for allowing us to photograph parts of this book in their homes.

A special thanks to Miriam Gourley, Tony Lydgate, Heidi Somsen, and Kim Streit for allowing us to include their beautiful shell art projects.

Table of Contents

Introduction

The secrets of the sea—they are tranquil, yet compelling; they are both mysterious, yet magical. There is something about the sea that calls to our very souls and sense of being. Perhaps it is for these reasons that seashells hold a fascination for all of us. What child has not picked up a seashell to hear the roar of the ocean? Tales of lost Atlantis and Neptune's Kingdom conjure images of castles with auger-shell pillars, visited by angelfish, starfish, and maybe even mermaids.

How we marvel at seashells found on mountain tops—evidence of an ancient sea or tectonic upheaval. Who can help picking up a shell that has washed up on the beach? How they attract us at gift shops in museums or seaside resorts.

Shells compel us just as the sea does. Man has been collecting, creating, and decorating with seashells for thousands of years. They come in hundreds of shapes, sizes, and colors. From ancient to modern civilization and throughout the world, shells such as abalone, mother-of-pearl, and coral are both treasured and coveted.

This shell was a gift; I did not find it. It was handed to me by a  friend. It is unusual on the island. One does not often come across such a perfect double-sunrise shell. Both halves of this delicate bivalve are exactly matched. Each side, like the wing of a butterfly, is marked with the same pattern; translucent white, except for three rosy rays that fan out from the golden hinge binding the two together. I hold two sunrises between my thumb and finger. Smooth, whole, unblemished shell, I wonder how its fragile perfection survived the breakers on the beach.

—*Anne Morrow Lindbergh, Gifts from the Sea*

Accent

y special passions that have always brought me hours of quiet joy, a sense of accomplishment, and something to treasure are sewing, photography, decorating, and collecting. Everyone I love knows how much pleasure each of these bring me; and on special occasions, and sometimes for no reason at all, they bring me gifts that are to become a new part of my passions.

For example, one sunny Tuesday morning after a visit to the seaside, my dear friend Kathy brought me a wicker tray crowded with treasures she had found during her travels. There were antique buttons made from mother-of-pearl, needle cases tucked inside tiny shells, and pretty little shells hidden among the pieces of lace. Each was an accent that would someday add a perfect simple touch.

I have been doing what most people only dream of doing, since 1981. It was then that I decided to focus my career and fill my days with my passions of designing, creating, photographing, painting, writing, and marketing. I have selected pieces from my collection of vintage laces and linens to sew beautiful original gowns for the loveliest of brides, and have spent many winter days as the proprietress of the Bearlace Cottage at the top of Main Street in Park City, Utah.

However, I began by designing and creating with my own collectible family of teddy bears. They, because of their loving ways and enduring charms, are what I am best known for.

Because making each new teddy bear was to become a career, it meant that I then must find them new homes. Selling them to collectors who would love them was easy, but it meant never seeing them again or being able to enjoy the quirky little tilt of their head or the magical gleam in their eyes. I decided early on that to always remember each and every one, I would paint them. I love watercolors as a medium, and to the pictures of my bears I have added bunnies and mice. I paint for myself, for family and friends, to sell, and as illustrations for children's books.

The last little while I have spent with my husband Bruce and my kitty Raisin, designing and authoring, visiting my four children, and playing with my nine grandchildren. Life is so full of unexpected promises that I look forward to each new day.

Anita Grane

Cache **of Shells**

Whenever I walk along the beach or visit the sea-side towns that I so dearly love, I add to my collection of shells. I can never resist the charm of their sweet scalloped shapes or unexpected textures.

I adore anything made from shells—whether it be old or new. Vintage pieces are truly my favorites because I know they have so many stories to tell, and because they offer endless ideas for making new pieces that look somewhat the same—almost but not quite.

One such vintage box, found on a rainy afternoon at a seaside antique shop, is this one which I now keep in my breakfast nook. It is kept here so that I can sift through the shells and begin to imagine new uses for each as I relax with Raisin and my afternoon tea.

Seashell *Sphere*

One afternoon, while sharing tea with Raisin, I decided that maybe I should use some of my antique silver serving pieces to display a new piece that I wanted to create with some of the shells I had collected. So I spent the last hours of the day gluing a multitude of tiny shells to a foam ball that I found in my box of odds and ends. I decided it was so simple, that one day when the grandchildren come, we can make one for each of them to keep or give to someone special.

I have found that craft glue and hot-glues make excellent adhesives for most seashells. Shells that are porous lend themselves well to craft glue. The hot-glues made for use on wood or jewelry have a stronger bond than the regular craft hot-glue. I used glue made for glass, jewelry, or other slick surfaces when working with polished shells.

Sweetheart Boxes

When a friend was sorting through her collections, trying to decide what to keep and what to give away, she came across a bag of shells she had been saving for so long she had forgotten where she had acquired them. She knew I collected shells, so she sent them to me. For her birthday, I decided to take some of the shells and make a small box to hold some of the things she had kept. I used translucent pearl gold acrylic paint, ceramic tile mastic, a papier maché box with a lid, and part of her collection of shells.

• Paint the entire box but not the lid and let it dry.

• Arrange your seashell design first on a work surface.

• Using a putty knife, apply a thin coat of mastic to the lid and sides, following the manufacturer's instructions.

• Using a fork, scratch grooves in the wet mastic.

• Gently press your seashells into the mastic. Let dry.

• Paint the entire lid and sides.

This antique heart-shaped box belongs to a friend of mine. She uses it in her studio where she surrounds herself with all of her favorite things.

She especially loves anything that looks very old, so she taught herself and me to "age" certain shells in my collection. Now, whenever I want to make something that has a vintage appeal, I simply take a paintbrush or rag and lightly cover the shells with an antiquing medium or a dark oak stain. After applying the first coat, I rub certain areas so that the stain is not evenly applied.

Mary Jo Hiney, an artist whose work in fabric is truly an art form, has created this delicate shell box with a soft satin lining that hides a tiny almond-colored pearl. She creates the boxes from pieces of lightweight cardboard, glue, and remnants of the fabric she so loves to collect. Handmade boxes such as these can be purchased in galleries that offer handmade pieces from juried artists, or can be made by following the instructions in Mary Jo's book Making Fabric-covered Boxes.

Mary Jo Hiney is one of those women who do not often come into one's life. She is truly one of the most talented and gifted artisans in the field of fabric arts in the world today. Her precision, her attention to detail, her sense of design and color, as well as her modesty and humility make her one of the rare few to which the word "artist" truly applies.

She is an inspiration to each of us who find it essential to surround ourselves with beautiful things that are created by hand and are unlike any treasured possessions owned by anyone we know. What we hold most dear must come from the heart and be part of all that which is in our very soul. To Mary Jo I say thank you for just being you and for sharing so much with all of us/.

Gingerbread Cottage

I covered a little wooden house planter I found in a garden store with a variety of tiny shells. They were attached with my hot-glue gun on each side of the door in a mirrored image.

Shadow Box

My friend Joanie used sandpaper as a unique and fitting backdrop for the shells in this purchased shadow box.

Seashell *Soaps*

These classic shell-shaped bath soaps are a must in my guest bathroom. Always popular, they can now be found in a wider range of sizes, shapes, and colors.

Perfect Placement

Careful positioning of these starfish on my vanity makes this scene come to life. It appears as though the starfish is on a morning stroll past a top shell and scallop.

Each shell has its own signature and its own story to tell. They are so much a part of so many individual lives—so much an expression of so many talents.

The small frame on the opposite page was made by my mother. The picture that it holds is one of her in younger romantic days spent with friends visited a long time ago in towns along the shore.

A more acclaimed artist than my mother is British-born Sarah Lugg. She creates in a mixed media of collected treasures, old and new, and lives and works with her husband in Hampstead London. She was raised in the beautiful countryside of the south of England, spending weekends and most holidays with her grandparents on the Isle of Wight. Her younger years spent beach-combing proved to have a great influence on Sarah's work today.

After graduating in Graphic Design from Kingston University, she spent her early twenties working as a designer for Sir Terence Conran. Sarah painted and worked extensively on her own style of collages during this time. She now devotes herself purely to her collages and paintings.

Sarah's innovative mixed-media collages are enriched by her unique personal interpretations. Her work combines the sophisticated delicacy of ancient Assyrian forms with a deeply sensitive use of color and exquisite finely judged textures. Nature is also a source of unending influence on her work. Her paintings take inspiration from the tiny details of texture, shape, and color also found in her collages. These transformed visions are given new dimensions as Sarah experiments with the relationship and proportions of images and backgrounds.

The unique and distinctive style of Sarah's work has led to many prestigious commissions and exhibitions. These include 30 collages for the British High Commission in Trinidad and 60 for the United Kingdom Mission to the United Nations in New York, as well as commissions from many interior design companies, art galleries, and private collectors worldwide.

Sarah is a regular exhibitor in the United States at Artexpo and Accent on Design, where her shows are always a sellout. Following this success, her work has been published in the form of boxed sets of art cards, journals, stationery, a range of fine art prints, and a collection of exquisite wire-edged ribbons.

When decorating my home, every corner is a showcase for my collections. Everything must be arranged just so—with attention paid to the finest detail. On the page opposite, I have arranged the unfinished mirror I am framing with shells, with my collection of boxes that hold the shells I am using. I simply can't put it away until I am finished—that may be a while yet. So, to make it look complete, until it actually is, I have carefully draped a piece of my grandmother's lace over the unfinished corner.

One day I will also repair the antique frame above. It is somewhere between a frame and a mat with shells delicately glued to cut cardboard. When repaired, I am going to hang it in my guest bedroom from a piece of vintage ribbon.

Above: Nubby shells contrast with the colorful smooth flower petals of a fragrant, spring bouquet.

Left: A touch of natural elegance was added to this wicker tray by simply gluing scallops and dainty seashells into the corners with a hot-glue gun. I use this as a desk set and the lovely mother-of-pearl pen when writing friends and family.

Above: This brass shell candleholder is also part of Susan Ure's childhood. It was purchased in a gift shop at the beach and now sits on a bamboo hall rack in the entrance to her garden room. Everywhere one looks in Susan's home, there are shells of every kind, size, shape, and color. They are as interesting and as diversified as she is!

Left: Friends are made in the most unexpected of places. The drawing hanging behind the orchid is a self-portrait of my new friend, Susan, when she was just a girl. I met Susan one day while browsing in her wonderful shop in Salt Lake City, she so appropriately christened Floribunda. It is filled with everything I love—from handmade jewelry to hand-painted pots. As we began to talk, we learned of each other's passions for collecting and she invited me to her home to share some of her collected treasures. In her guestroom where her granddaughter sleeps is her drawing with a potted orchid filled with shells she collected on her trips to Catalina Island as a child. Those afternoons were ones she loved more than any other, so her home is filled with the memories that were collected on the beach and lovingly stored all of these years.

Shells fill your home with light, elegance, and the soothing sound of the sea.

One seashell is simplicity itself. When gilded with gold it can be a study in elegant femininity—a finishing touch of art to an everyday piece. A collection of shells can be as strikingly beautiful as delicate oriental orchids when gathered together to fill a family heirloom pedestal plate.

Seashells are often found treasures that create fond memories, or they can be the final touch that adds the charm to hours spent in the company of one's own thoughts and dreams.

This simple flower arrangement is given added charm with the addition of shells and white beans to the vase. A smaller glass vase may be added to the large vase to contain water for fresh flowers.

Seashells are the perfectness and harmony of nature and when sur-rounded by bath oil in a heart-shaped bottle that is then sealed with wax, invite you to relax in a peaceful world of your own. The addition of a smooth dog conch evokes visions of a seaside visit that brings the promise of tranquility and renewal. For it is the sea that brings to the mind's eye waters that wash away cares and salty breezes that awaken the senses.

Painted Seashells

Petite and colorful, these dainty shells were painted with a white pearlized acrylic paint before the tiny flowers and were added.

When I began looking for ways to decorate with seashells, it seemed as if all of my friends had become collectors overnight. These pictures were taken in the home of Dixie Barber who is a dear friend that loves collecting as much as I do. In her home, her shells take on more of a safari tone, surrounded by handmade baskets and vintage bottles of either brown glass or those covered in rattan or wicker.

When decorating with seashells, you should not only be guided by traditional shades of white and vibrant shades of blue, but by shades of the golden yellow of late afternoon. For a colleague of mine, Joanie Howell, who surrounds herself with the colors of the garden, I made a set of starfish that are adorned with jewels of vibrant color. She keeps them on a serving tray in her spare bedroom as an unexpected surprise for invited overnight guests.

I needed a very special gift for much loved friends, so I painted the church in which they were married on the sides of this wooden box. The trees are an artist's interpretation, but the shells are indicative of Hawaii where the church is located. Not only do the shells act as a finishing touch, but I adhered them with hot glue so that they can also act as a handle. Inside the box, I placed the pictures and the mementos saved from my friend's wedding day.

On my travels, I have collected cases that were much used to travel long ago, in days when the journey was as grand as the destination itself. I cannot even imagine putting them in a closet for occasional use, but use them, instead, for a nightstand by the side of my bed. On top, I place my favorite reading lamp, which is a bit on the whimsical side, and those shells which hold the most memories for me. At night when I read or turn out the light, I imagine myself in a place far away, sharing the days with those I have envisioned from the pages of my favorite novels.

Opposite: The fun of flea-market decorating is using something intended for a special purpose for something else. I love to travel, especially to the sea. A day of serenity spent on the beach, gathering enough shells to fill my suitcase on the trip home, is what heaven must be like to me.

Top Right: When you are a collector, "too much is never enough." I have my shells everywhere you can imagine in my home. In my dressing room is a very plain wooden knickknack box which is filled with tiny treasures. If you look very closely, you will see my tiniest shells tucked away in places you might not have guessed.

Bottom Right: There are as many ways to use shells as there are artists to create them. This curtain tieback, which was originally designed to be a necklace, was created by Ginger Sizemore. When she sent the necklace for inclusion in another publication, I had to borrow it to photograph as any decorator might have imagined.

Opposite: This piece of wearable art is more often admired hanging on the wall in the bedroom of my dear friend Kathy Pace than it is while it is being worn. Fashioned from treasures that create fond memories; flea-market finds that "were calling her name"; snippets of vintage lace, antique quilts, and embroidered ribbons, this piece was created as a perfect addition to her wardrobe—even if only for sentimental reasons.

Below: When entertaining family or friends, each detail must be complete. I would never consider setting a table without touches of linen, handcut crystal, and delicate treasures. The pristine white of this elegant piece of coral is an addition that has the charm a Victorian lady might have added in the style of her own time.

Kathy Pace creates exquisite fashion and home accessories, using vintage laces and fabrics; so it is not surprising that she would also incorporate antique shell buttons into her designs. Her home reflects her talents in delicately stitched pillows, lace flutters at each window, antique dolls reclining in vintage wicker prams, and chairs accompanied by antique bears. Gooseberry Hill Notions is Kathy's own line of patterns and bear-making supplies.

Her sewing room is a delight indeed—accented with an antique ribbon cabinet and spools of thread in a myriad of soft colors. It is in this space where lovely christening gowns and exquisite vests are created.

Created by Sarah Lugg

Drawer Pulls

When exploring the sands of the sea, shells are often spotted that must be used as additions to pieces of art. Sarah Lugg uses each of her finds in the collages she designs (opposite); but I use mine for more practical accents such as these drawer pulls on my jewelry chest. Either way, both are loved and admired daily.

I used small assorted shells, including smooth, round cowries and rough conch shells, along with craft glue, a rotary tool, and a ⅛" dowel.

• Using your rotary tool, cut the dowel into 1" long pieces.

• Drill holes for the dowel in drawer where the pulls will be located. Test holes with the dowel for a snug fit.

• On one side of each shell, drill a hole for the dowel, testing the holes for a snug fit as well.

• Apply a drop or two of glue into each hole in the drawers and shells.

• Insert a dowel into each drawer hole. Push a shell onto each remaining dowel end.

There is a room in my home in Park City where I sit in the golden light of the late afternoon to do that which I love to do—whether it be writing a note to a friend far away, reading a book that has been left on the shelf much too long, or sorting through the pieces of art I have saved in drawers and fabric-covered boxes.

In this quiet corner, there are touches from some of my collections. There are tiny shells that are delicately colored, like fading antique silk; there are pieces of pristine white linen, lace that lets the colors of the day whisper through, and, of course, fresh flowers gathered from a walk down a shaded mountain path.

Upper right: I have taken some of my favorite tiny shells and, with my glue gun, attached magnets or push pins to the backs of them so they can be used to hold my notes, pieces of art, or a sentimental thought I do not want to forget.

Lower right: Nothing ever seems to be "finished" for me. Everything needs one more touch of something very special. For example, I found this wicker letter holder at a garage sale and I immediately came home and added a few shells—now it "fits" in the place where I embrace the quiet pleasures of late afternoon.

We wake in the same small room from the deep sleep of good children, to the soft sound of wind through

the casuarina trees and the gentle sleep-breath-
ing rhythm of waves on the shore. We run bare-
legged to the beach, which lies smooth, flat,
and glistening with fresh wet shells after the
night's tides. The morning swim has the nature
of a blessing to me, a baptism, a rebirth to the
beauty and wonder of the world. We run back
tingling to hot coffee on our small back porch.
Two kitchen chairs and a child's table between
us fill the stoop on which we sit. With legs in
the sun we laugh and plan our day.

—*Anne Morrow Lindbergh,*
Gifts from the Sea

Fantasy

find myself, when surrounded by the waters of the sea, in a world that is created only by me. It is one filled with imagination and fantasy—where reality is only what I wish it to be. It is a wonderland in which mermaids exist, where lovers are carried home from far off places, and where treasures are buried deep beneath the sands. During these times of solitude and imaginings, I become not only an artist but a writer—a creator of words and pictures that tell not only my stories, but the stories of those I love. Was it someplace by the sea that Lewis Caroll wrote Alice in Wonderland? Was it here that he created all of the make-believe characters and the fantasy?

One afternoon when redecorating my dressing room for the coming days of spring, I designed an entrance to make the place I spend every morning as fanciful and fun as a cottage by the sea. My little gift tags, which were inspired by the pieces created by Sarah, have watercolor letters painted from a stencil, little shells and flowers glued to each one, and they so appropriately read "Welcome to Wonderland". Because I smile each time I pass by my "work of pen and art," it is proof positive that each room in my home must have a tiny bit of fantasy inspired by my days by the sea.

Opposite: Whimsical ornaments and children's books are also among those things which I collect. I try to read at least one book each day to help me remember to always be a child at heart. Each night after I read aloud to my grandchildren, my husband, or my cat Raisin, I place the book on my bedstand with my favorite ornaments and a small "flower" arrangement given to me by a friend.

Right: I once bought a large bag of shells at a flea market and could not decide what to do with them—so I put them away for another time. Then one day while reading to my granddaughter, the illustrations in the book inspired me to make a series of fanciful trees—and, of course, the shells I had been saving were perfect. We painted cardboard cones and covered them with shells. With the two of us laughing and remembering and making up stories as we went, it made an afternoon that both of us will remember for a long time to come.

What could be as inspired as the pages of a child's book if it isn't the decorations for our homes at Christmas? I love them both—children's books and decorating for Christmas—they are not only for children, but for the child in all of us—who, if we are truly blessed, will live as long as we do.

Because I love the sea and all that it is, I often decorate my home for the holidays with that which I have collected from the ocean myself, or been given by family and friends from the things they have collected. These little angel ornaments are especially dear to me because they were made by my granddaughter. She sculpted the head from sculpey clay, then glued seashells together for the bodies and wings. The lights were made by my friend Tricia Dalglish. The instructions for re-creating them are on page 134. Simply choose smaller shells when making the strands for holiday decorating.

Lower left: Making the wrapping of a gift as special as the gift itself makes the giving as memorable as the receiving. I personalize all of my paper and cards with a seashell stamp. Usually, I use brown ink for a nostalgic tone. And as unromantic as it seems, I use my computer, greeting card software, and color printer to scan drawings like the ones I have included here. I copy and paste the scan on an 8½" x 11" document and card, then print. I, of course, then tie my packages with hand-dyed silk ribbons—the color of the sea—or raffia, if the gift is for a man; and glue shells on top to replace the bow

Spired Birdcage

One day I was rearranging my collection of shells and I made a somewhat surprising discovery—I had glued shells to almost everything I own, and these little houses were no exception. Somehow a piece just does not seem to be complete if the edge is not adorned with shells; or the front door seems somewhat uninviting if not surrounded by the gifts of the sea.

Seashell *Bird*

A thing of nature is something to treasure—it is the epitome of art. To create one of nature's tiniest, most beautiful beings with another of nature's wonders is a simple pleasure in which I indulge as often as I possibly can.

I created this dainty creature with three small scallop or wing-like seashells; black, blue, and light brown paint; heat-set polymer clay; a hot-glue gun and glue sticks; a #4 paintbrush; and a papier maché egg.

- Form clay into a ball for the bird's head. Pinch one side of the clay ball and shape it for a beak.

- Bake the clay head, following manufacturer's instructions. Let cool.

- Glue your shells to the egg for wings and a tail, then adhere the clay head to the large end of the egg.

- On a protected work surface, paint the entire bird light brown. Let dry.

- Using the paintbrush, spatter the body (not the head) with black paint. Spatter the body with medium blue.

- Paint a black stripe around the neck for a collar. Paint another stripe with medium blue. Paint the eyes and beak with black.

Above: I made this tiny duck for a friend whose husband is an avid watcher of birds. Its body was molded from polymer clay and its wings are small, yet perfect, turkey wing shells.

Opposite: Any collector will come to cherish the writings and poetic "paintings" of Sarah. The charm of her collages cannot be resisted by anyone who loves the "collected little things" that evoke memories of wonderful times spent in magical places with unforgettable friends. Each one so different, yet somewhat similar; each with its own memory to retell, its own pictures to repaint.

Created by Sarah Lugg

Victorian Pincushion Box

I made this pincushion years ago from pieces of vintage lace. As with everything as time passes, I decided it needed something new—a little addition of shells maybe—attached to the tiny threads that hang from the top. They can be easily removed if I tire of them and want to add something else.

Decorative Plate

Over the years, my grandmother's china has become chipped and cracked beyond repair. Because I treasure them so, I have lovingly mended each one with tiny shells that mean almost as much to me as my grandmother's china.

Mosaic *Coffee Cup*

This "oversized" coffee cup was found at an art festival in Laguna Beach and was made by local artist, Lygia Dubin. Its one seashell was enough to bring it home as part of my collection. It is so delightful that I use it daily for everything—it truly makes me smile as it whispers children's tales of fantasy and make believe.

Seashell Kingdom

A family day at the seashore—time together, carefree days, finding new surprises. Unexpected treasures like these small shells and this tiny sandcastle are gathered together by children and given as gifts in appreciation for days long remembered.

My home is crowded with shells. Brimming with their poetic charm, naive appeal, and sheer fantasy. So, too, are the homes of my friends who love the sea and all of its offerings as much as I do.

Upper left: This small fountain filled with shells belongs to a friend of mine. During the long summer days, she keeps it on her "southern-style porch;" but during the long months of winter, it rests next to her desk. She loves the sound of water and finds the soothing qualities of shells from the sea and running water are helpful while she spends countless hours working at her desk.

Lower left: The birdbath with the seashell rim is in my backyard. I must admit that I constructed it for the photo shoot, but it has become one of my favorite pieces of shell fantasy.

Opposite: My editor is certain that this wonderful angel with the shell wings, created by artist Heidi Somsen, watches over her home. Someday when she has her own cottage on the beach, it will hang just inside the front door to welcome and protect all who enter there.

It is true that the sea seems to beckon to everyone of all ages; but it also seems to be an undisputed truth that its most powerful fascination is with children and lovers. As either walk along its sandy shores, listening to the sound of the waves and feeling the wind upon their cheeks, they daydream of wishes made, yet still unfilled, of moments not yet cherished, and of fantasies still unimagined. They collect their shells along the way, carry them home in pockets and handbags, and make them into something for someone they hold near to their hearts. It is amazing to me how simplistic or how intricate and beautifully detailed each painstakingly created keepsake can be.

Right: The shell wind chime was made by my friend Joanie's granddaughter. Each shell was thoughtfully elected and carefully arranged so that the gift would be long- and lovingly treasured.

Opposite: This sailor's valentine was fashioned by Tony Lydgate, a much respected author and woodworker, to resemble those made by sailors long ago and carried home to wives and girlfriends in days when not only was the sea more treacherous but just a little more romantic, as well.

To those who say that earthly possessions are meaningless, I offer my gifts from the sea. The shells I collect inspire me with their beauty, humble me with their simplicity, teach me with their imperfections. Their presence connects me with my past, their soothing sound of the ocean brings me peace, their uncomplicated magnificence seems to put everything in perspective.

Out onto the beach for the afternoon where we are swept clean of duties, of the particular,

of the practical. We walk up the beach in silence, but in harmony, as sandpipers ahead of us move like a corps of ballet dancers keeping time to some interior rhythm inaudible to us. Intimacy is blown away. Emotions are carried out to sea. We are even free of thoughts, at least of their articulation; clean and bare as whitened driftwood; empty as shells, ready to be filled up again with the impersonal sea and sky and wind. A long afternoon soaking up the outer world.

—*Anne Morrow Lindbergh, Gifts from the Sea*

Focus

While on a solitary walk along the water's edge, I often stop for awhile at the house of a friend. She is a woman who knows exactly what she likes—lace-edged antique linens, chintz quilts made with a fine hand, blooming violet pots covered in tiny starfish, and delicate mismatched pieces of vintage china. Whenever I enter her weathered gray cottage, my eye is forever drawn to a different certain something. As I visit, I always find myself focusing on one special object again and again. Invariably, at some point during our conversation, I finally apologize and ask my friend about it. From then on, the conversation flows to memories of the past and hopes for the future.

That upon which we focus is usually something collected, something treasured, something intriguing. Whether beautiful or ugly, dominant or subtle, whimsical or classic, whatever catches our eye is also what usually nourishes our spirit and feeds our soul.

Seashell Flowerpot

A treasured bag of shells can make as many variations of this flowerpot as there are afternoons in a year's time. To start any design on any afternoon, you will want to begin with a porous flowerpot, premixed grout, a putty knife, a utility sponge, seashells, and acrylic spray varnish.

• Using a putty knife, apply grout about ¼" thick to the outside of the flowerpot. The thickness of the grout is dependent on the size of shells used.

• Press shells into the grout until the entire flowerpot is covered. You may reposition the shells while grout is still wet.

• Using a damp sponge, wipe off the excess grout from the shells and let it dry.

• Spray the flowerpot with varnish and let dry.

Long after the sun sets and the waters turn a midnight blue, I want the light and the warmth of the day to linger. I always light the outside of our cottage by the water with candles. Because the wind often blows, the candles are put into flower pots that have seashell motifs on the outside and are filled with sand. The ones shown here were designed by Jill Grover, who loves the ocean, dime-store decorating, and is always using the unexpected. She even made a shell garland for the table from large shells with tiny holes drilled to string the ribbon through.

Our favorite time to visit the beach is when the summer crowds have long departed and there is room again for the townspeople who have lived along the shores most of their lives. These are the afternoons when the true enchantment of the sea unfolds a tapestry of riches that nourish not only my emotional well-being, but my artistic soul.

Opposite: It was shortly after one of these visits that I was at home in my work room on a rainy afternoon—longing for the sunlight on the water and the ocean breezes in my face. It is so easy to re-create our days at the beach by simply designing pieces that are marked by sunlight and sunny patterns. I had never designed on tile before, but I sat down and sketched out a pencil design on an unsealed piece of terra-cotta tile. I then painted a leaf green water-color wash over the design. I spilled out my seashell collection onto the table and sorted through them, selecting the perfect shells for the petals, leaves, and vase. Once the shells and starfish were hot-glued onto the sketched design, I applied an acrylic varnish over the tile and shell surfaces to protect them.

Right: One misty morning at the shore, while we were browsing through the now emptied antique shops, I found this beautiful old basket made from shells. It was different than any I had seen before and when I inquired, the shopkeeper could not remember where he had gotten it. It didn't matter, really—I loved it without knowing any of the stories it had to tell. It now sits on a shelf in my guest room filled with other treasures collected from the sea.

Left: I made this paperweight to keep my important papers from blowing through my open window. It was made by applying mastic over a glass ball and pressing assorted shells into the mastic.

Below: I don't believe this comb and brush set is ever actually used. It was given to a friend of mine by someone who is very dear to her. When I saw it for the first time, it became an inspiration for me to create a collection of my own beautiful items for my dressing table. It had never occurred to me to brush my shells with gold and silver paint, but the effect is one of elegance.

Seashell *Mirror*

All through my home there are frames and mirrors that I have created with the shells I have collected or been given. They are among my favorite pieces —especially when they are centered around an old mirror that is beveled and etched. A piece like this is less complicated than it appears. You simply need about 32 oz. of ceramic tile mastic, a fork, a mirror with a wide wooden frame, premixed cement repair, a putty knife, and seashells. If you want to give the mirror an antiqued look, you will also need oak-colored wood stain and a rag.

- Use the fork to scratch grooves in the entire wooden frame around mirror. Be certain to retire the fork from food use.

- Use your putty knife to apply a thin coat of mastic to the frame. Next, use your fork to scratch grooves in the mastic before letting it dry.

- Arrange your seashell design first on your work surface. Then, using the putty knife and working on 3"–4" of frame at a time, apply the cement about ¼" thick. The cement will set up quickly, so you may want to practice on a separate surface first.

- Gently press your seashells into the cement, working from inside to outside and keeping all seashells pointing in the same direction. Repeat this until the entire frame is covered. Allow mastic to dry.

- Optional: Using a rag, apply stain to the shells to create an antique effect.

Framed *Surf*

Tiny Shells *Frame*

Seashell-edged Frame

I like new things—those that are still perfect with nothing missing and nothing cracked or broken. I also like the feel of wood that is smooth and has the touch of glass when you rub your hand across the top of it. But what I love most is that that which is aged and weathered, and shows the imperfections of time and love and use.

Weathered *Surf Frame*

This frame is not one of mine, but was made by a friend of mine. She had saved some pieces of wood she had found so long ago that she couldn't remember from where. Make your own frame from weathered wood or use a 1½"–3"-wide weathered wooden frame, blue-gray and white acrylic paints, craft glue, a #6 paintbrush, a scrap of paper, several favorite seashells, and an old toothbrush, you can create this unique frame.

- First arrange seashells on the frame and then glue in place.

- Paint the edges of each shell with blue-gray paint. Gently wipe away the wet paint with a scrap of paper, leaving the shells slightly stained where paint was.

- Cover the seashells loosely with paper and spatter-paint the frame, using the toothbrush and white paint.

Created by Sarah Lugg

Frame *with* Seashell Accents

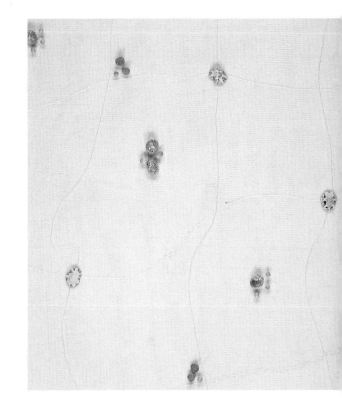

Not all of the frames that adorn the walls in my house are filled with pictures. Many are simply hung because they are pieces of art in and of themselves. Someday I may add a favorite family photograph, but for now they are enjoyed just as they are.

The idea of this frame occurred to me on the same day I designed the shell tile on page 78. I decided to make a frame that looked like clay and this was the end result. To make this frame you need a 2½"–3"-wide wooden frame, cream-colored acrylic paint, clear acrylic varnish, antiquing medium, a 1" flat paintbrush, a pencil, putty knife, rag, seashells, and tile grout.

- Using the putty knife, apply grout ½" thick onto the front of the frame, then press shells into grout as desired.

- Using a pencil, draw a design into the grout and let it dry.

- Paint the frame, being careful not to paint seashells. If paint gets on the shells, wipe them off with a damp rag. Allow the paint to dry.

- Using a rag, lightly apply antiquing medium to the entire frame and let dry.

- Using the paintbrush, apply varnish to the entire frame.

Opposite: When making preparations for an outdoor seafood feast, I wanted the decorative elements to speak of the ocean. I strung delicate starfish and shells together and draped them over chairs, leaving impressions of seaside tidepools.

Below: One of my favorite adornments is simply to string tiny shells on beading elastic and/or glue larger seashells onto a variety of napkin rings to complement my outdoor table setting or my favorite china.

Above: Because the ocean is not at my doorstep, I find every opportunity to invite the ambiance of the beach by adding shells to my favorite planters.

I have a dear friend who is a woman with an eye for elegant touches. As a gift one year during the holidays, she brought me this fabric-covered box. She was certain that I would fill it with letters, photographs, and sketches of art that evoke enduring images and sentiments of the past. Since I received this gift, I have made many more—not only for myself, but to give as gifts. You need only to cover a papier maché box with fabric and secure a shell to the top with a hot-glue gun.

I was making several projects for this book, and by the time I did this mirror and frame, I had become a little "shell crazy."

In my favorite movie "Enchanted April" Lottie talks about the villa in Italy being a "tub of love." I still love that line, so I used my tiny shells to write this message on the antique mirror in my bedroom. It is as perfect a statement for me as it was for Lottie!

Also on my nightstand are several of the treasures that I love the most. They change, of course, on a weekly basis because change is something that is important to me. When a favorite piece is placed somewhere new it reminds me of things I had forgotten and acts as a new echo from days spent long ago.

Blue *Embellished* Box

I love little boxes because they hold so many important "little things." I have them everywhere and they are that which I love to give as gifts most of all. This blue box is one of my favorites, not only because of the shells and the color, but because of the beads—they add a slight twinkle and transparent color to the subtle shading of the shells. The box was made by using blue acrylic paint, beads, craft glue, a cameo, a #6 paintbrush, seashells, varnish, and a wooden box with a lid.

* Paint the entire box (not lid) with blue. Let it dry.

* Apply varnish to the painted box, following manufacturer's instructions.

* Working in small areas at a time, apply the glue to the lid.

* Press shells and beads into the glue, covering the top and sides of the lid.

Marked by sunlight and sunny patterns, this dressing room is a sanctuary for myself and any weekend guest. It is easy to see that I cannot seem to simplify any room in my home—to me, too much is never enough. Whenever there is a tiny open space on a wall or dresser top, it must be filled with treasures that I love. I have so many—treasures that is—and I simply cannot bear to put them away where they are not enjoyed and may even be forgotten. So I stack them one on top of each other, I layer them, I hang them, and every time I have a minute, I move them around. Most of my "things" are found treasures, gifts from family and friends, and things I have made—which is why I love them out—everywhere—where I can enjoy them, touch them, and remember everything there is to love about them.

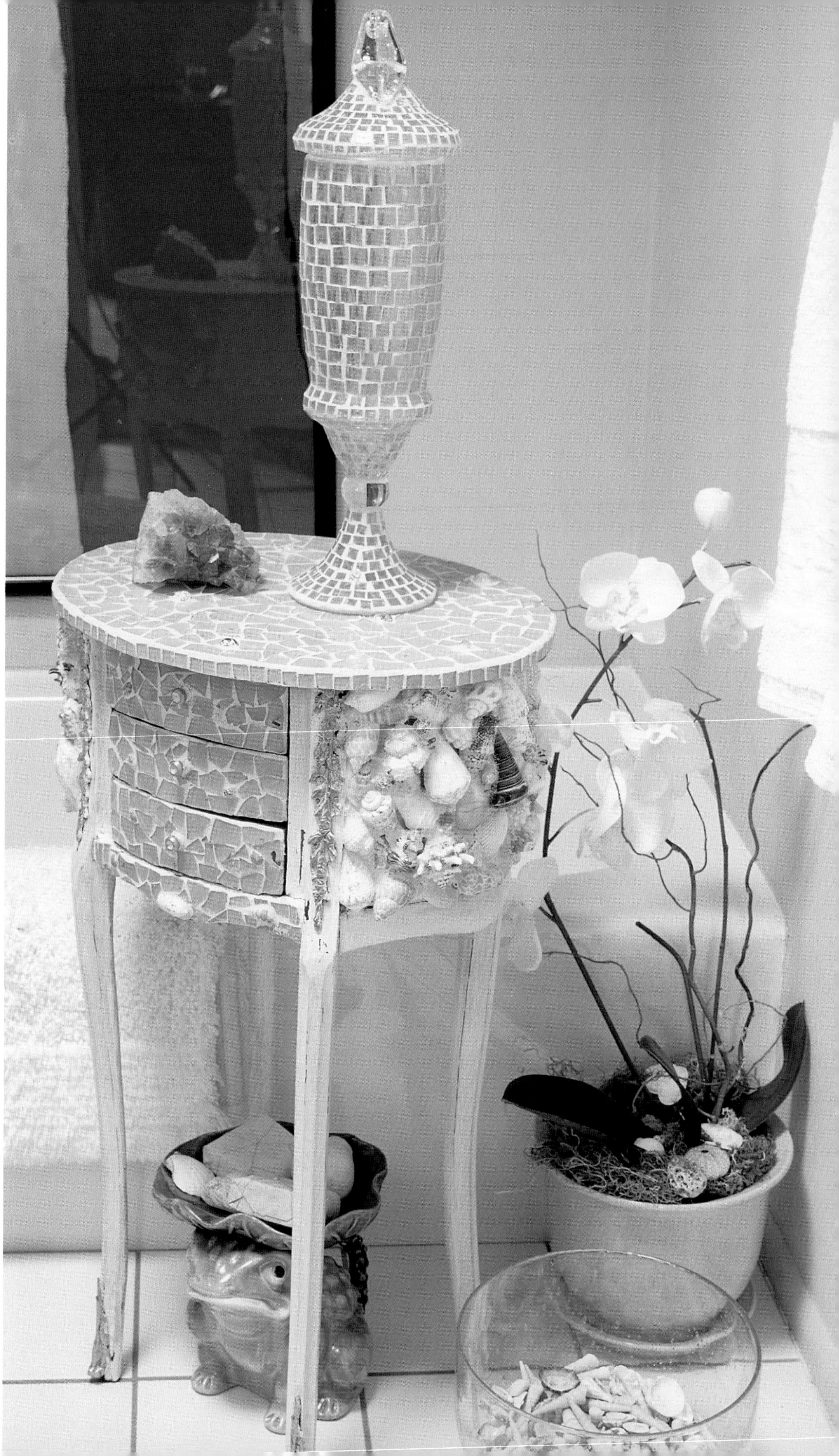

Seashells and mosaics have become a much used medium among artists today and it is true that one of the most accomplished in this field is Ercole, Inc. Showroom. The pieces created here are truly unbelievable works of art. These are several pieces that are among those in the collection of Susan Ure.

Left: In direct contrast to the elaborate magnificence of Susan's pieces are these simple glass decanters filled with whatever one fills jars in a dressing room. The jars were purchased in a small gift shop in Park City and I made the labels on my computer. Some of the bottles I actually use, and some are meant only to sit and be pretty.

Right: Glass domes are being used for everything from decorating to covering delicate flowers in the garden. This dome was found in the home of Miriam Gourley, where she was photographing it for her new book The New Paper Style. *She cut a paper edge and temporarily glued it to a pedestal cake plate. She then added a small flower arrangement, a starfish, and the dome. It is very appealing in its simplicity and could be easily changed for each new season or holiday.*

Like flowers gathered along a walk down shaded country paths and carried home to make bouquets that fill a cozy country home, seashells gathered during an early morning walk while the sky is still pink from a newly rising sun make any home seem more sentimental and sweet. Simply wash the seashells thoroughly, then pour them into a favorite container—it is the simplicity that will make these one of your favorite things.

Because it is the simple small touches that make family and guests feel special in a guest bath, try stacking the towels on a tiny chair so they are easy to find and much more charming than hanging on a "towel bar."

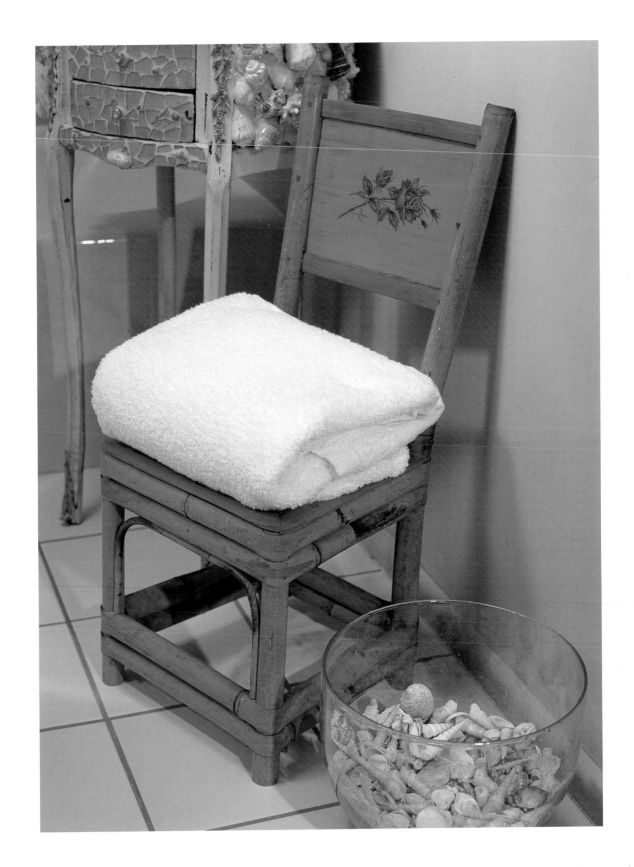

One cannot
collect all the
beautiful

shells on the
beach. One
can collect
only a few, and

they are more beautiful if they are few. One moon shell is more impressive than three. There is only one moon in the sky. One double-sunrise is an event; six are a succession, like a week of school-days. Gradually one discards and keeps just the perfect specimen; not necessarily a rare shell, but a perfect one of its kind. One sets it apart by itself, ringed around by space—like the island.

—Anne Morrow Lindbergh, *Gifts from the Sea*

illuminate

Late in the afternoon when the light turns a golden hue, even the ocean begins to be lulled into tranquility; and then late afternoon inevitably leads to the growing peacefulness of the evening hours. Inspired hours that are used for reading in the company of only oneself, engaging in conversation and sipping fine wines with friends, or sharing hopes and dreams with family and loved ones.

The light of the afternoon is so different from the subtle yellow that shines from the fire or from underneath the handmade shades in every corner of my home. The lights that shine from inside the home softly, very softly, echo the personalities of the people who live inside. They must be sometimes understated, sometimes overdone, sometimes vintage, sometimes contemporary, but always personal and always enchanting.

That which sets a mood—which is a subtle refined finishing touch—can be glass shades with bohemian-style shells hanging with beads and baubles; it can be shells filled with candles and woven in tiny fiber nets; or it can be floating candles among freshly picked flowers. Whatever it is that sends forth light in a darkened room is there to be a small beacon to light the memories of the past, the hopes for the present, and the dreams of the future.

This wonderful bohemian-style lamp shade was created by Phoebe Lantini Design. It is one of my favorites among Susan's collection of eclectic art. The unexpected combination of glass and shells, contemporary and natural, feminine yet stainless is a contradiction that is wonderful.

Opposite: Everything should be enjoyed and not always for the purpose it was intended. These treasured silver candlesticks with their tiny birds were the perfect place to display my favorite shells. Where the candle should have been placed, I simply hot-glued my shells. These remind me of something that might have been in the seaside palaces of royalty who lived in a gentler time when small things seemed more delicate and more coveted somehow.

Upper: My home is filled with the collectibles that friends have given me and those that I have gathered myself. This small light is not so very special, but it is one I especially treasure. The lamp base was given to me by a friend, the shells were glued on by my grandchildren, and I made the shade. It is a collective piece created by not only myself, but those around me who take the time to remember what I love.

Lower: In the evening while I sit by my window and read I can hear the music from my neighbors house—it seems to reach everywhere through the summer nights. I find these times when nothing special happens to be among my favorite and those I most remember. Maybe not each evening individually, but remembered collectively because of the restful, peaceful sensations that so totally surround me and fill my very soul.

Left: This candle was created by pouring wax into a favorite shell I found on one of my early morning walks. I then set the shell in a tiny woven bag that I had tucked away in one of my linen boxes.

Opposite: Floating candles create a mood that is enjoyed not only through the winter months but the summer ones as well. For a small gathering of friends that I was having, Kim Streit filled this glass candleholder with white beans, shells, and fresh flowers I had gathered from my garden. This last particular touch of inspiration cannot be left much later than the hours spent entertaining, due to the absorption of water by the white beans.

Shell-embellished Candle

In a home where the potpourri-scented rooms are lush with inspiration, candles are essential. And they cannot be just ordinary candles randomly placed, but candles that are as varied as the visitors who come into this room to stay awhile.

The candle on the lower right is decorated by using craft glue, a craft stick, dried flowers, low-temperature glue gun and glue sticks, a pillar candle, a variety of seashells, and Spanish moss.

- Using a craft stick, evenly coat the bottom two-thirds of candle with craft glue. Press moss onto the glued area and let it dry.

- Using your glue gun and beginning with the largest flat seashells, apply glue to the inside shell edges and adhere to the moss-covered area.

- Add remaining shells, filling in the open spaces.

- Adhere small dried flowers between the shells.

Sunday tea—with cinnamon toast, Gifts from the Sea, *and my grandchildren all around me—is the time I relish the most. It can be the morning we first arrive at the beach or the day we are leaving; either way, it always seems that as we look up, there is just a whisp of a white cloud that is the only adornment in the blue July sky. And in the peace of the evening sunset, we all gather around the table to candlelight and tiny gifts that were always left by someone unknown to surprise us. It is no wonder that these are the days that hold the charm of childhood regardless of our age. They were moments filled with the pleasures of doing nothing, joyous hours meant to indulge only oneself, carefree afternoons that beckon like old friends all the days of our lives. These were the days that were guarded by angels, marked by sunlight, and meant to be remembered as one of the true uncomplicated pleasures in an otherwise complicated lifetime.*

The waves echo
behind me.
Patience—
Faith—
Openness, is
what the sea has

to teach. Simplicity—Solitude—Intermittency . . . But there are other beaches to explore. There are more shells to find. This is only a beginning.

—*Anne Morrow Lindbergh, Gifts from the Sea*

Theme

So essential to a sense of being complete is a central or pivotal theme, that I believe EVERYTHING must have a theme, whether it be the stories in children's books, a shower given for a bride-to-be, or the way you choose to decorate your home. It is little wonder that anything created without a central theme is either discarded, unattended, or neglected.

One of the pleasures of creating anything is the development of its theme. It is oftentimes created when you are totally unaware; but it need always be there, beckoning like old friends.

In a town visited long ago, one of my mother's friends gave to me this wonderful teapot. On the trip home, the spout was broken. Because I often use vintage dishes as the center of my created themes, I used pieces of coral and tiny shells to repair this much treasured piece. I am certain that I love this piece even more now; it is as strikingly beautiful as the summer blossoms that fill my garden.

Left: It matters not whether your daily napkins be pure linen touched with embroidery or squares torn from vintage fabric. That which will take them from ordinary to extraordinary is eclectic silver napkin rings gathered through the summer months enhanced with a tiny shell. It is the tiny touches that are always most remembered.

Right: "Make something from nothing," my mother would say to me. That way you will always have whatever you want. One afternoon in late fall, I began to think of the months of winter and the early sunsets followed by hours of darkness. I wanted a set of new candlesticks so I purchased the discarded ballisters from a junk store, drilled a hole in the top, and I was finished. To complement these candlesticks, I cut the remaining ballisters in half and glued them to an old picture frame before inserting a mirror. This is a perfect setting for a beautiful shell dish.

It is amazing to me that wherever you travel in the world, you seem to be attracted to those treasures to buy and bring home that all look like they were made to go together. These three pictures are part of Susan Ure's collection. The shell orchid pot was purchased "a long time ago," during one of her trips to Mexico. The hat was purchased in Katmandu where they visited before they began their trek to the Himalayas, and the oriental chest and goddess were purchased in Laguna Beach. Each brings her back to the days she spent walking along the beach in quiet solitude, dreaming the dreams that fill a child's head. Each of these found riches, lovingly carried home with great care, act as a beacon from the past. Each time she walks into a room and spots them, dusts around them, or moves them to a new place, they bring back all of the memories of where she was and who she was with, as if they were the pages in a photo album.

Table *Centerpiece*

In the late summer months, it is time to beckon old friends, share the early sunsets, and gather round an intimate seaside table set for dinner. To make the meal, one must follow the recipes of their favorite chef, but to make the centerpiece, one must use their imagination. Designer Kim Streit used dried beans, dried moss, a floral oasis, floral pins, either artificial or fresh-cut flowers and foliage, scissors, seashells, assorted sizes of starfish, and a tray large enough for the oasis.

- Soak the oasis in water for about 30 minutes and place the saturated oasis in a tray on the work surface.

Plastic wrap, rather than a tray, may be used to protect the work surface.

- Pin moss over the entire oasis.

- Cut flowers to approximately 4" and pin the flowers and foliage over moss.

- Arrange the beans, seashells, and starfish in center of oasis.

A small dinner party can be a time of understated spectacle and surprise that will stir your very soul. It is a time of charmed hours spent in the company of those that can be casual acquaintances you would like to know better, those you know that capture your imagination, or friends you hold most dear.

Deep *Scallop* Lights

An eye for elegant touches, her view of a world touched by fantasy, seeing only sentimental reasons as being what is important is why my friend Tricia Dalglish has such a grand passion for all she does. For her, a quiet little dinner with friends is like the pages out of an Alice in Wonderland chapter. Here she created a wonderland of her own with lights, using a strand of size C-7 bulbs, two deep scallops for each bulb, and a hot-glue gun with jeweler's glue sticks.

*   Adhere one scallop to strand with flat edge of shell along cord and concave side of shell against bulb. Make certain to use hot glue along entire flat edge of scallop and use enough hot glue to cover the cord.

*   Adhere a second scallop on the opposite side of the bulb, matching flat edges of both scallops. Then just hold together until the glue hardens.

In the hands of individual artists, each shell has its own signature; but what is common to them all is their perfectness and harmony with nature.

Top Right: This shell wreath was created by a friend of mine to hang on her door and welcome guests on the misty mornings early in the season.

Bottom Right: These gift bags are as special as the gifts they contain. Whenever Kim Streit gives a gift, she gathers all of her found treasures from the sea and designs her packages as if they were the gift itself.

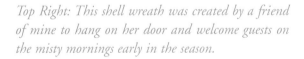

Ginger Sizemore is an artist whom I have yet to meet, but who graciously and trustingly sent her piece to include in my book. Ginger is originally from Colorado, but now lives with her husband Sherman and their exotic parrots and macaws on a macadamia nut farm on the Big Island of Hawaii.

When she was a child, she was fascinated with two things—her mother's button box and her father's collection of seashells, accumulated during his navy days. These two elements sparked her interest in jewelry making, and as a child, Ginger would make necklaces and sell them on consignment in local shops.

When Ginger completed high school and business school, she had the opportunity to move to Hawaii, where she began her own seashell collection and continued to create jewelry and wearable art.

Ginger fulfilled her dream of owning her own store in which to sell her creations. She retired from owning and managing eight unique shops after sixteen years.

Currently, Ginger teaches jewelry making and continues to create one-of-a-kind art, which she supplies to local boutiques and galleries.

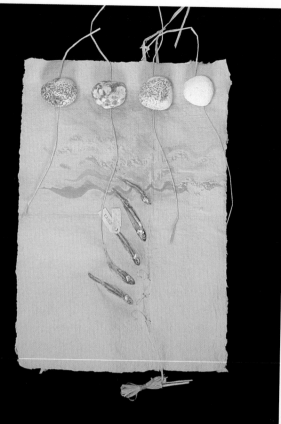

One of the wonders of the shells collected from the sea is their ability to be used anywhere, at any time, for almost any purpose. Sara Lugg uses tiny shells to adorn the gift bags she gives to family and friends. It is a part of her "signature" and her special way of making something ordinary, very extraordinary. In the days of summer, I fill all of the pots on my porch with shells. Not only does it help to keep the moisture in during our hot Utah summers, but they add a bit of mystery and romance to my garden. This large smooth dog conch shell can be used to decorate any time of the year. This shell is perfect for winter decorating in the mountains of Park City when placed on an old wooden sleigh with my penguin and collected pinecones. If you walk from my front porch, through the rooms of my house, and out onto the terraced deck behind our home, you are apt to find shells in almost every place that you could possibly imagine—and some you probably couldn't!

Created by Sarah Lugg

Metric Conversion Table

Inches to Centimetres

cm—Centimetres

inches	cm	inches	cm	inches	cm
1/8	0.3	10	25.4	31	78.7
1/4	0.6	11	27.9	33	83.8
1/2	1.3	12	30.5	34	86.4
5/8	1.6	13	33.0	35	88.9
3/4	1.9	14	35.6	36	91.4
7/8	2.2	15	38.1	37	94.0
1	2.5	16	40.6	38	96.5
1 1/4	3.2	17	43.2	39	99.1
1 1/2	3.8	18	45.7	40	101.6
1 3/4	4.4	19	48.3	41	104.1
2	5.1	20	50.8	42	106.7
2 1/2	6.4	21	53.3	43	109.2
3	7.6	22	55.9	44	111.8
3 1/2	8.9	23	58.4	45	114.3
4	10.2	24	61.0	46	116.8
4 1/2	11.4	25	63.5	47	119.4
5	12.7	26	66.0	48	121.9
6	15.2	27	68.6	49	124.5
7	17.8	28	71.1	50	127.0
8	20.3	29	73.7		
9	22.9	30	76.2		

oz—Ounces
g.—Grams
16 oz. = 1 lb.

Lbs—Pounds
Kg.—Kilograms
1,000 g. = 1 Kg.

Solid Measures
Ounces to Grams & Pounds to Kilograms

oz.	g.	oz.	g.	Lbs.	Kg.
1	28.35	12	340.2	7	3.175
2	56.7	13	368.55	8	3.629
3	85.05	14	396.9	9	4.082
4	113.4	15	425.25	10	4.536
5	141.75	Lbs.	Kg.	11	4.99
6	170.1	1	.4536	12	5.443
7	198.45	2	.907	13	5.897
8	226.8	3	1.361	14	6.350
9	255.15	4	1.814	15	6.804
10	283.5	5	2.268		
11	311.85	6	2.722		

Index

index